LEBANON

...in Pictures

Visual Geography Series®

LEBANON

...in Pictures

Prepared by
Geography Department

Lerner Publications Company
Minneapolis

Courtesy of UNRWA

In the Beirut refugee camp of Burj al-Barajneh, a young girl stands in the ruins of bombed-out buildings.

This book is an all-new edition in the Visual Geography Series. Previous editions were published by Sterling Publishing Company, New York City. The text, set in 10/12 Century Textbook, is fully revised and updated, and new photographs, maps, charts, and captions have been added.

Website address: www.lernerbooks.com

LIBRARY OF CONGRESS CATALOGING-IN-PUBLICATION DATA

Lebanon in pictures

(Visual geography series)
Rev. ed. of: Lebanon in pictures / Camille Mirepoix.
Includes index.
Summary: Lebanon's topography, history, society, economy, and government are concisely described, augmented by photographs, maps, charts, and captions.
1. Lebanon. [1. Lebanon] I. Mirepoix, Camille. Lebanon in pictures. II. Lerner Publications Company. Geography Dept. III. Series: Visual geography series (Minneapolis, Minn.)
DS80.E84   1988   956.92'04   87-25997
ISBN 0–8225–1832–5 (lib. bdg.)

International Standard Book Number: 0–8225–1832–5
Library of Congress Catalog Card Number: 87–25997

VISUAL GEOGRAPHY SERIES®

Publisher
Harry Jonas Lerner
Associate Publisher
Nancy M. Campbell
Senior Editor
Mary M. Rodgers
Editors
Gretchen Bratvold
Dan Filbin
Assistant Editor
Kathleen S. Heidel
Illustrations Editor
Karen A. Sirvaitis
Consultants/Contributors
Dr. Ruth F. Hale
Isaac Eshel
Sandra K. Davis
Designer
Jim Simondet
Cartographer
Carol F. Barrett
Indexer
Sylvia Timian
Production Manager
Gary J. Hansen

Independent Picture Service

A hall in the palace at Beit al-Din shows the geometric detail of Arabic design.

Acknowledgments

Title page photo courtesy of UNICEF.

Elevation contours adapted from *The Times Atlas of the World,* seventh comprehensive edition (New York: Times Books, 1985).

5   6   7   8   9   10   –   JR   –   03   02   01   00   99   98

Ballet dancers perform against the backdrop of Roman ruins at Baalbek, located in the foothills of the Anti-Lebanon Mountains.

Contents

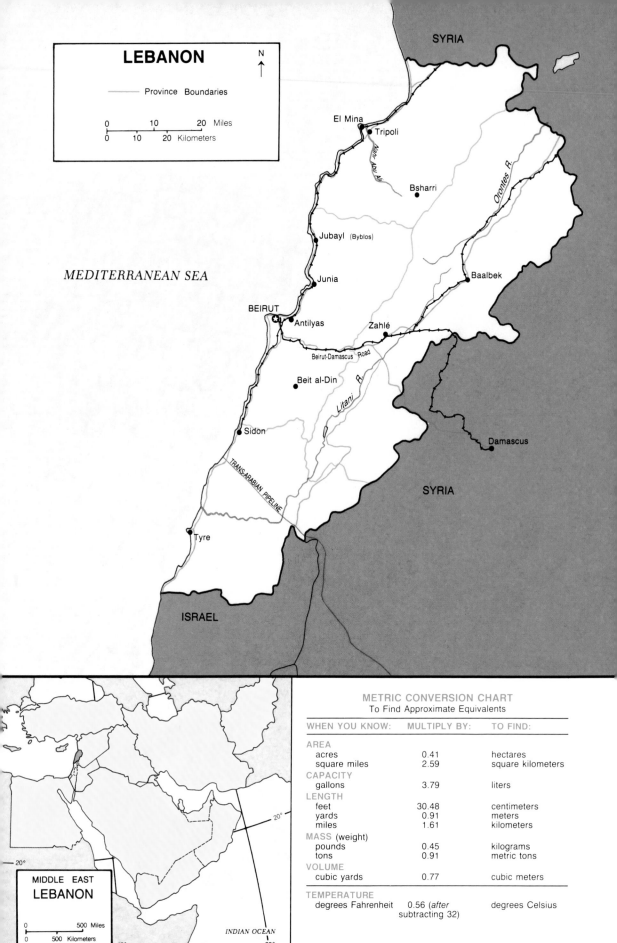

LEBANON

N

Province Boundaries

0　10　20　Miles
0　10　20　Kilometers

SYRIA

El Mina
Tripoli

Nahr Abu Ali

Bsharri

Orontes R.

Jubayl (Byblos)

Junia

MEDITERRANEAN SEA

Baalbek

BEIRUT
Antilyas

Zahlé

Beirut-Damascus Road

Beit al-Din

Litani R.

Sidon

TRANS-ARABIAN PIPELINE

Damascus

SYRIA

Tyre

ISRAEL

MIDDLE EAST
LEBANON

0　500 Miles
0　500 Kilometers

20°

20°

40°

60°

INDIAN OCEAN

METRIC CONVERSION CHART
To Find Approximate Equivalents

WHEN YOU KNOW:	MULTIPLY BY:	TO FIND:
AREA		
acres	0.41	hectares
square miles	2.59	square kilometers
CAPACITY		
gallons	3.79	liters
LENGTH		
feet	30.48	centimeters
yards	0.91	meters
miles	1.61	kilometers
MASS (weight)		
pounds	0.45	kilograms
tons	0.91	metric tons
VOLUME		
cubic yards	0.77	cubic meters
TEMPERATURE		
degrees Fahrenheit	0.56 (*after* subtracting 32)	degrees Celsius

Lebanon's coastal highway passes the Ramlet el-Beida district of Beirut, the nation's capital city.

Introduction

Although Lebanon became an independent republic in 1943, it has been a meeting place where civilizations have overlapped for 5,000 years. For example, the Canaanites —some of whom were later known as the Phoenicians—settled the land in about 3,000 B.C. and developed Lebanon into a crossroads of trade. As a result of its long commercial history, many peoples, languages, beliefs, and cultures have mingled in Lebanon over the centuries.

With a large Christian population, Lebanon is unique among Middle Eastern countries, where most people follow the Islamic religion and are called Muslims. The contrast between the Islamic Eastern and the Christian Western way of life presents a serious conflict that the people of Lebanon have yet to solve. The arrival of thousands of Palestinian refugees—a result of the hostilities between the Jewish state of Israel and the Arab world—has created additional pressure on Lebanon's political and economic life.

Once the commercial, intellectual, and financial center of the Middle East, Lebanon suffered a destructive civil war during the 1970s and 1980s. A cease-fire was arranged in 1989, and an international agreement rewrote Lebanon's constitution. But Lebanon is still plagued by deep religious rivalries, and the country's weak economy is posing a new threat to a long-sought peace and to political stability.

Many villages have grown along the mountainsides of the Lebanon range, the highest reaches of which are typically covered with snow.

1) The Land

Lebanon lies at the eastern end of the Mediterranean Sea and includes more than 4,000 square miles of territory—an area that is slightly smaller than the state of Connecticut. A roughly rectangular strip of land bounded on the north and east by Syria and on the south by Israel, Lebanon is 135 miles long and 20 to 55 miles wide.

Two mountain ranges that are parallel to the Mediterranean coast dominate Lebanon's landscape. The mountains have influenced Lebanon's history by providing refuge for the inhabitants from many outsiders who have tried to overpower them. Lebanon's location on the Mediterranean coast also has shaped the nation's develop ment by giving the people of the region access to sea trade with Africa, Europe, and Asia.

Topography

Four topographical regions make up Lebanon—the coastal plains, the Lebanon Mountains, the Bekaa Valley, and the Anti-Lebanon Mountains. At their widest the coastal plains are only eight miles across, and in places where the mountains drop steeply into the sea, the plains disappear altogether. The fertile land and the navigable bays of the coastal plains provide ideal locations for Lebanon's major cities.

The bay at Junia reveals the kind of coastline that has encouraged the establishment of Lebanon's many port cities.

The Bekaa Valley lies between the Lebanon and Anti-Lebanon mountains. Fruits, vegetables, and grains grow in a patchwork of fields that yields much of Lebanon's food supply.

The Lebanon Mountains form the coastal range and rise sharply, following the shoreline from the Syrian border down the entire coast to the mouth of the Litani River. The highest peak in the country—Qurnet al-Sauda—lies in northern Lebanon near the city of Tripoli and reaches an altitude of 11,024 feet. The mountains decrease in height from north to south.

The Bekaa Valley, a plateau 75 miles long and 5 to 10 miles wide, separates the Lebanon Mountains from the Anti-Lebanon range. This central region is part of the Great Rift Valley, which was formed by the giant fault in the earth's crust that runs from Syria to southeastern Africa. Within Lebanon, the rift forms a narrow plain from 2,500 to 3,000 feet above sea level. Although the Bekaa Valley receives less than 10 inches of rainfall per year, rivers irrigate the land, enabling farms in the region to produce plentiful crops.

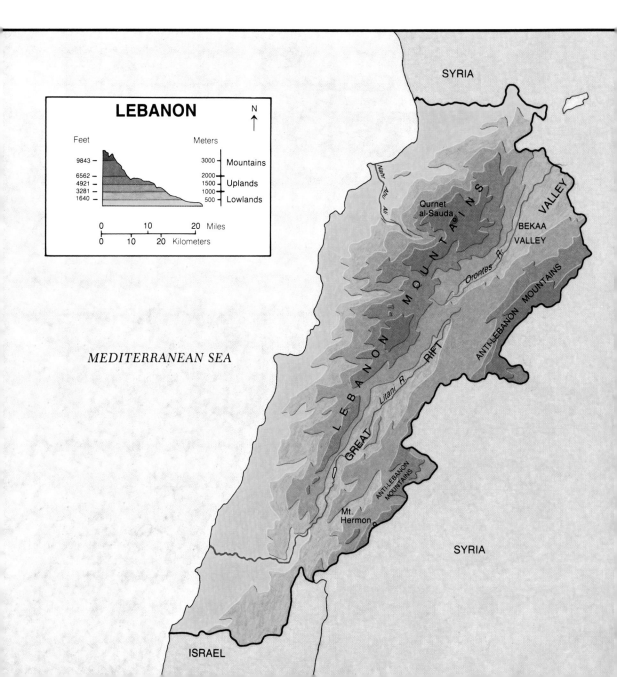

Lebanese women tend a plot of vegetables in the fertile Bekaa Valley.

The Anti-Lebanon Mountains lie in the interior of the country and extend into Syria and Israel. The highest peak in the Lebanese section of the range is Mount Hermon (9,232 feet), which straddles the southern border between Lebanon and Syria.

Rivers

Two major rivers run the length of Lebanon, providing irrigation water for farming.

The Litani River begins in the Bekaa Valley near the ancient town of Baalbek and flows southward before cutting through the Lebanon Mountains. The waterway empties into the sea just north of Tyre. The Litani River also produces hydroelectric power, the result of a development project begun in 1957.

The Orontes River flows from the northern part of the Bekaa Valley northward into Syria. Many other rivers in Lebanon are seasonal. They flow in the spring when

The Anti-Lebanon Mountains mark Lebanon's western boundary with Syria. Flanking the Bekaa Valley, the snow-covered mountains water the plain below when warm weather melts the ice.

mountain snows melt, filling the once-dry streambeds with water.

Climate

Lebanon's summers are long and hot, with little rainfall. The coastal regions receive humid Mediterranean air, and many Lebanese who live in port cities visit the mountains to find relief in the coolness of higher altitudes. In the summer, the temperature hovers around 90° F at sea level, and winter temperatures along the coast average 56° F. Temperatures are usually 20 degrees lower in the mountains, although the Anti-Lebanon Mountains are semi-arid.

Most of Lebanon's rain falls in January and February, during the winter rainy season. The country gets about 40 inches of rainfall per year. Much of the precipitation in the mountains falls as snow. Since the most frequent winds come from the Mediterranean Sea in the west, the Lebanon

Independent Picture Service

Weather systems blow in from the Mediterranean Sea, bringing moisture that falls as snow in Lebanon's mountainous regions.

Mountains absorb the first impact of incoming weather systems and, to some extent, shield the Bekaa Valley and the Anti-Lebanon Mountains. Consequently, the Bekaa Valley receives less rain and must depend on the melting of winter snow for much of its moisture.

Flora and Fauna

For centuries the cedars of Lebanon were harvested so that foreign kingdoms could construct palaces from the tree's sturdy, scented wood. As a result, few cedar groves remain, although the cedar remains the national symbol of Lebanon. The Lebanese people are attempting to reforest their country with cedars and other trees, such as oak, maple, and juniper. These efforts beautify the country and increase the lumber supply. Newly planted trees also preserve the soil, because the tree roots prevent the topsoil from eroding. Eight percent of Lebanon is forested.

In the heavily cultivated coastal region, native plants include poppies and

Independent Picture Service

When summer comes and melting snow floods Lebanon's small streams, children take the opportunity to fish the seasonal pools in the lowlands.

During the hot summer months along Lebanon's Mediterranean coast, water skiers find relief at Pigeon Rocks near Beirut.

and pine cover the highlands. In the high plain of the Bekaa Valley, which is nearly treeless, various wild herbs—mostly of the daisy and pea families—are interspersed with thorny shrubs.

Deer live in the mountains, and smaller animal species include polecats, hedgehogs, and hares as well as squirrels and other rodents. An unusual mammal is the hyrax, which is about the size of a house cat. The hyrax looks like a rodent but is actually a hoofed creature whose nearest relative is the elephant.

Flamingos inhabit the marshes of the Bekaa Valley, along with pelicans, ducks, and herons. All of these birds are migratory, flying south in the autumn and north in the spring. The higher elevations support many smaller birds, such as cuckoos and woodpeckers, as well as falcons, kites, and other birds of prey. Insects, especially occasional swarms of grasshoppers, are common. Eels, bass, and mullet are among the fish found in Lebanon's rivers.

anemones (a kind of buttercup) and trees such as tamarisk and buckthorn. Along with cedars, stands of olive, fir, cypress,

The largest remaining group of Lebanon cedars *(left)* are at Bsharri. Olive groves *(right)* grow on the lower slopes of the Lebanon Mountains. The olives are picked for food or are crushed to produce olive oil for cooking.

This aerial view of Beirut was taken before warfare caused large-scale destruction to the city. During the civil war, much of Beirut's shipping industry was transferred to less-damaged port cities along the coast.

Up-ended garbage containers block a roadway in the uninhabited zone—sometimes called the Green Line—between East and West Beirut. Now dismantled, the Green Line separated the Christian and Muslim sections of the city.

Cities

Because it has been a trading region since ancient times, Lebanon has several port cities with long and varied histories. Beirut, Tripoli, Sidon, Tyre, and Byblos are all several thousand years old and have gone through many transformations. Eighty percent of Lebanon's population live in urban areas.

BEIRUT

Rising on the hilly coast against the background of the Lebanon Mountains is the capital city of Beirut. A trading center as early as 1500 B.C., Beirut has since been one of the chief ports of the region.

Over the centuries, Beirut blended European and Arabic influences and produced both brisk commercial activity and opportunities for leisure. Homes and businesses are situated a few minutes away from splendid beaches and only 30 minutes from the mountains, where temperatures are cooler. Between 1952 and 1975 the city was a center for construction, commerce, food processing, textiles, shoes, and publishing businesses.

Although it is barricaded with sand-bags, this transit station in East Beirut is still open for business.

In the mid-1970s, however, internal strife in the south led to civil war that left deep scars on Beirut, as well as on other cities and villages in Lebanon. The violence caused damage in housing, trade, and public services. Although the population of the city fell during the war, Beirut has returned to its pre-war population of 1.5 million.

During the civil war, Beirut was divided into a Christian eastern section and a Muslim western portion. This division created a barren no-man's-land known as the Green Line in the middle of Beirut. Although the Green Line no longer exists, bombings and other terrorist activities caused immense damage to the city, especially in West Beirut.

Several refugee camps within the city of Beirut do not have adequate supplies of safe drinking water and food, nor do they possess sufficient sewage facilities. These refugees try to cope with reestablishing their makeshift dwellings after a period of intense fighting in 1986.

15

SECONDARY CITIES

With 500,000 inhabitants, Tripoli is the second largest city in Lebanon. Modern Tripoli consists of the port district of El Mina on a small peninsula and the city proper, which lies two miles inland. The Nahr Abu Ali, a stream that enters the sea east of El Mina, further divides the city. Tripoli is an important seaport and railway destination, and, after completion of a petroleum pipeline from Iraq, the city added oil refining to its economic activities. Tripoli, like Beirut, suffered damage during the civil war, and parts of the city were left in ruins.

Zahlé, with 200,000 people, is Lebanon's third largest city. About 50 miles from Beirut, on the slopes of the Anti-Lebanon Mountains, this flourishing resort and market city is known for its flowers, vineyards, and cascading mountain streams. The city is also a major hub for Syrian troops that began operating in Lebanon under the guidance of the Arab League, an association of the heads of Arab countries whose goals are to strengthen Arab ties and to address Arab concerns.

Sidon, a small city of 100,000 people in southern Lebanon, serves as the administrative hub of the region and as a shipping

The name Tripoli combines the Greek root words for three *(tri)* and for cities *(poli)*. Once three distinct settlements, Tripoli now consists of a port and a business area.

Independent Picture Service

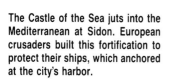

The Castle of the Sea juts into the Mediterranean at Sidon. European crusaders built this fortification to protect their ships, which anchored at the city's harbor.

Independent Picture Service

Jubayl (ancient Byblos), once the capital of the Phoenicians, is now a small fishing port on Lebanon's Mediterranean coast. The town's walls and ruined fortresses date to at least 1200 B.C.

center. The Castle of the Sea, built by European crusaders in the thirteenth century, stands at the entrance to the port. The ruins of the Castle of St. Louis and ancient tombs are visible relics of Sidon's past. Since 1948 Sidon has been a home for many Arab refugees from Palestine, the region now governed by Israel. The civil war of 1975 caused a great deal of destruction, and, occasionally, the government has lost control of Sidon to Palestinians who live in the city's refugee camps.

ANCIENT SITES

Tyre (population 70,000), the southernmost city in Lebanon, is built on a small, rocky coastal outcropping of land that was an island in ancient times. Castles and ornate cemeteries are evidence of its former greatness as a center for talented builders and artisans. Excavations have revealed a buried city that was paved with colorful mosaics.

Byblos (modern Jubayl), which residents claim is the oldest town in the world and which may date back as far as 3000 B.C., contains Phoenician tombs, temples, and protective walls from around the twelfth century B.C. Located 20 miles north of Beirut, Jubayl is a small city, yet at one time it was the commercial and religious capital of the Phoenicians.

Baalbek was originally founded in honor of the Canaanite god Baal. After taking over the region in the first century B.C., the Romans built their own structures on the site, including the now-ruined temple dedicated to the Roman deity Bacchus.

The Roman sun god, Helios, is depicted on this sculpture at Baalbek. During Roman times the city was called Heliopolis and was the site of a winter resort.

Baalbek is one of the oldest sites in Lebanon with architectural remains. This small town in the foothills of the Anti-Lebanon Mountains grew into a winter resort area in Roman times when its name was Heliopolis—"City of the Sun." The vast ruins include an acropolis (hilltop temple), an early Christian church, and imposing temples to the Roman gods Bacchus and Jupiter.

At one time, Baalbek's Temple of Jupiter had 54 columns supporting its roof. Now only 6 of the pillars of the colonnade remain standing.

Archaeological investigations of Byblos (modern Jubayl) have unearthed ruins of former civilizations. One of the world's oldest cities, Byblos has been continuously inhabited for nearly 5,000 years.

2) History and Government

Lebanon's western territory corresponds closely to that of ancient Phoenicia, a region composed of independent trading cities. Around 3000 B.C. a people called the Canaanites occupied what is now Lebanon. They became known as the Phoenicians, a name taken from the Greek word for the purple dye that Canaanite traders made from sea mollusks. By about 1500 B.C. the main cities of Phoenician civilization were Byblos, Sidon, Tyre, and Beirut. Each was important for its seafaring, commercial, and religious activities.

Phoenicia

Although the Phoenicians spread their civilization throughout the ancient world, they never had a unified state. Rivalry among the independent cities kept them apart, and none of them was strong enough to subdue the others and to achieve the unity needed to form a nation.

Phoenicia extended as far north as the town of Ruad in Syria and was bounded on the south by Mount Carmel (now in Israel). On its eastern flank were the Lebanon Mountains, and to the west lay the Mediterranean Sea. The location of Phoenician cities on the Mediterranean coast and the high mountain range that separated these cities from the plains of the interior determined the seafaring destiny of the Phoenicians. The ports of Byblos, Ruad, Sidon, and Tyre became dominant trading cities, with Sidon and Tyre eventually becoming the strongest commercially.

Contact with Egypt

The Phoenicians and Egyptians had a long history of trade. To the Egyptians, who lived in the treeless Nile River Valley, the hardwoods that the area of Lebanon offered were precious. Archaeological investigations of the Egyptian pyramids have uncovered wooden funeral barges, coffins, and furniture made from Lebanese cedar. The Egyptians traded gold and metalwork for this special building material.

The trade between the Egyptians and Phoenicians continued for hundreds of years until the Hyksos, invaders from central Asia, introduced horse-and-chariot warfare into the territory. At the beginning of the sixteenth century B.C., these newcomers dominated not only Phoenicia but Egypt as well. The Egyptians overcame the Hyksos by the early fifteenth century B.C. and established an Egyptian kingdom that included the region of present-day Lebanon.

From about 1500 until the mid-1300s B.C., Phoenician city-states were under Egyptian rule. Then the Hittites, an Indo-

These second-century A.D. ruins of an aqueduct (water-carrying passageway) are at Tyre, one of the preeminent trading centers of Phoenicia.

When archaeologists discovered the burial site of the Egyptian Pharaoh Tutankhamen in 1922, his tomb contained furniture made of Lebanese cedar.

The Phoenicians covered their wooden ships with pitch to make them watertight. A third-century B.C. slab shows the ships with a single sail and rear oars for steering.

European people from Asia Minor (mainland Turkey), extended their power southward into Syria and Lebanon. They were eventually overthrown in the mid-1200s B.C., when Egypt again reestablished its influence in Phoenicia

Phoenician Trade

When the Egyptian Empire began to decline in about 1200 B.C., the trading cities of Phoenicia entered a 300-year period of increasing independence and prosperity. During this time, the Phoenicians built fine sailing ships out of cedarwood and developed the art of navigating the seas by using the stars to guide them. The Phoenicians traded their lumber, fruits, perfumes, glass, pottery, and metalwork with merchants in a wide area surrounding the Mediterranean Sea. Royalty throughout Asia, Africa, and Europe clothed themselves in garments made from fabrics transformed by Phoenician purple dye. Phoenician traders brought back silver, gold, tin, linen, and other goods.

Perhaps the most important achievement that the Phoenicians shared with the world was their development of the 22-letter alphabet, which they used to keep trade records and eventually to communicate with foreign merchants. Phoenician navigators fully explored the Mediterranean and brought to European shores the inventions of their civilization. Pioneers in naval warfare and merchant sailing, the Phoenicians also directed their efforts toward the conquest of coastal areas in North Africa and Spain.

The Phoenicians occupied islands that could easily be defended, establishing markets on them that drew merchants from much of the world. The Phoenicians colonized parts of the islands of Cyprus and Rhodes near present-day Turkey and finally crossed the Black Sea. They founded Tarshish, a commercial colony on the coast of Spain, and Carthage in North Africa. The ancient Greek historian Herodotus recorded that the Phoenicians reached Greece, Italy, and Malta and that they sailed around the northwestern coast of Africa.

Independent Picture Service

A carving of an Assyrian soldier in a royal procession for King Sargon II dates from the late eighth century B.C. Sargon's reign signaled the height of the Assyrian Empire, which included the Phoenician city-states.

Courtesy of James H. Marrinan

A silver tetradrachm coin—issued in 323 B.C., the year Alexander the Great died—shows the head of Hercules *(top)* on the front. The back *(bottom)* depicts Zeus (the strongest of the Greek gods) enthroned, holding a royal scepter and an eagle. The Greek lettering translates as "Alexander the king."

Foreign Invasions

The Assyrians (from the northern area of present-day Iraq) ended the Phoenicians' independence. Assyrian invaders sought an opening for trade on the Mediterranean and subdued the Phoenicians in the ninth century B.C. By the beginning of the sixth century B.C., the Babylonian Empire (in the southern part of present-day Iraq) had held Phoenicia for 60 years. From 538 to 333 B.C. Persians ruled the Phoenician states. As each foreign power approached, Phoenician cities quickly offered tribute (payment) to the new rulers in order to avoid destruction. The Phoenicians cooperated with their conquerors but looked for ways to continue trade and to regain their independence.

The Greeks under Alexander the Great overthrew Persian rule, and Alexander was welcomed by all the Phoenician cities except Tyre, which eventually was conquered after a seven-month siege. After Alexander's death, none of his followers was strong enough to control the entire kingdom. Phoenicia became the object of the struggle between these leaders, until the Romans came on the scene in the first century B.C.

The Roman and Byzantine Eras

The period of Roman rule, which lasted from about 50 B.C. to A.D. 636, was a very prosperous era for the region that has become Lebanon. The area grew in population and contributed greatly to Rome's treasury and culture.

The Romans administered Lebanon and Syria as one unit. Tyre, Sidon, and other coastal cities accepted Roman rule. Many civic and religious leaders studied in Beirut, whose school of law became an important intellectual center in the Roman Empire. During this time, the region lost

Courtesy of Sona Karentz Andrews

With the Roman occupation of Lebanon, many builders in the territory began to use Roman architectural designs. The colonnade of the Temple of Bacchus at Baalbek shows classic Roman form.

Independent Picture Service

The advent of the horse and chariot—depicted in a carving from around 650 B.C.—revolutionized the nature of warfare. A charioteer's increased mobility gave him an overwhelming advantage over enemy foot soldiers.

much of its Phoenician identity and became more Roman in its intellectual, economic, and cultural development. Cities adopted a Roman style of architecture, building temples, stadiums, bathhouses, and villas after Roman models.

The Christian religion, which Jesus founded in nearby Palestine, had communities in Tyre and Sidon in the first century A.D. By the end of the second century some Christians were studying at the law school of Beirut. The Roman authorities persecuted Christians in Lebanon as they did elsewhere in the empire, but these persecutions stopped when the emperor Constantine established Christianity as an official religion in A.D. 313. Maronite Christians—a sect named after Saint Maron—developed a strong community in the Lebanon Mountains in the fifth century.

A portrait (top) of the Roman emperor Augustus, whose realm included present-day Lebanon, appears on a commemorative copper coin minted in A.D. 14, the year of the emperor's death. Around the rim are the words *Divus Augustus Pater,* meaning Divine Augustus Father. On the back of the piece (bottom) is a Roman temple and the word *provident,* suggesting that the Roman gods looked favorably on Augustus's reign. The letters *S* and *C* stand for *Senatus Consulto,* indicating that the coin, called an *as,* was struck with the authority of the Roman senate.

Spurred on by their zeal for the new religion of Islam, Muslim soldiers left Arabia in the early seventh century A.D. and conquered much of the Middle East, including Lebanon.

The Umayyads—the first Muslim dynasty—established forts throughout their newly conquered regions in the Middle East. Ruling from their capital in Damascus, Syria, the Umayyads made extensive use of local leaders to administer their territories. This Umayyad fortress still stands in Jordan, south of Lebanon.

Gradually, the eastern part of the Roman Empire developed its own identity. By the beginning of the fifth century A.D., this eastern section, which came to be known as the Byzantine Empire, had become independent. The Byzantine Empire controlled the province of Syria, which included the territory of Lebanon. Byzantine administration fell prey to corruption, which left the empire open to attacks from Arabs who sought to establish themselves in the eastern Mediterranean region. Arabs gained control of the Syrian portion of the Byzantine Empire in 636 and ruled the region until 1085.

Arab Control

Territorial expansion—prompted by the emergence of the religion of Islam in the seventh century—brought Arab armies to Lebanon from Arabia. Founded by the prophet Muhammad, the new religion encouraged conversion and colonization of neighboring peoples.

Within 30 years of Muhammad's death, conflict erupted over succession to the Islamic leadership. Two branches of Islam, the Sunni and the Shiite sects, developed. Sunni Muslims accepted the elected succession of caliphs (religious leaders) who have led Islam since Muhammad's death. The Shiites, on the other hand, contested the way leadership emerged. Shiites believed that only descendants of Muhammad's family should lead Islam and rejected the caliphs unrelated to the prophet.

After a period of struggle within Islam, the Umayyad dynasty—a Sunni group—gained control. They ruled the growing Islamic Empire from their capital in Damascus, Syria, for about 100 years. The Umayyads obtained the cooperation of the Lebanese in administering the region. The new rulers used the Byzantine system that was already in place and allowed local leaders to keep their status. The Arabs also made use of the great shipbuilding skills of the Lebanese to establish a strong navy.

Courtesy of Catholic Near East Welfare Association

The peoples conquered by the Muslims gradually began to speak Arabic. Even the Maronite Christians used the language, as evidenced by this dedication stone outside a Maronite church.

Another leading Arab family—the Abbasids—took control of the caliphate (the Islamic leadership) after the Umayyads weakened. Islam became more entrenched in Lebanon under Abbasid rule, and Arabic became the chief language. Some Lebanese Christians, particularly the Maronite group, maintained their religious identity throughout this period by isolating themselves in the Lebanon Mountains.

The economy grew substantially under Arab control. By shipping glass, textiles, cedarwood, and pottery throughout the Mediterranean area, Lebanon's coastal cities became prosperous again. This period also saw continued intellectual growth, and Lebanese scholars made contributions in philosophy, law, and medicine.

During the Abbasid dynasty, groups of Christian soldiers known as crusaders began arriving from Western Europe, especially from France. They made attempts

Courtesy of *Aramco World*

Maronite Christians fled to the mountains to escape their enemies and to practice their religion. Their churches became the focus of the community and often stood in the center of the village.

This well-preserved crusader castle stands near the town of Batrun in northern Lebanon. The castle is situated on a small piece of land that is backed by the steeply rising Lebanon Mountains in the east and that falls into the Mediterranean Sea in the west.

27

to conquer the territory known as the Holy Land, where Christianity had begun. In Lebanon the Christian soldiers captured Tripoli, Beirut, Sidon, and Tyre in the early twelfth century. The crusaders re-Christianized a portion of the Lebanese population and especially strengthened ties with the Maronite Christians. The crusaders defeated the Abbasids by the middle of the thirteenth century.

This brief period of crusader control ended when the Mamluks—who ruled Egypt at that time—defeated the Europeans at the end of the thirteenth century. Originally brought to Egypt as soldier-slaves from central Asia, the Mamluks took control of the Egyptian sultanate and extended their realm northeast to include present-day Lebanon and Syria. The Mamluks remained in power until the beginning of the sixteenth century.

The Ottomans

The Ottoman Turks, a central Asian people, conquered Syria and put an end to

Courtesy of Cultural and Tourism Office of the Turkish Embassy

A drawing of Tripoli done during the late Ottoman period shows the crusader castle of Saint Giles that overlooks the Nahr (river) Abu Ali. As the waterway flows into the Mediterranean Sea, it divides the city into two parts.

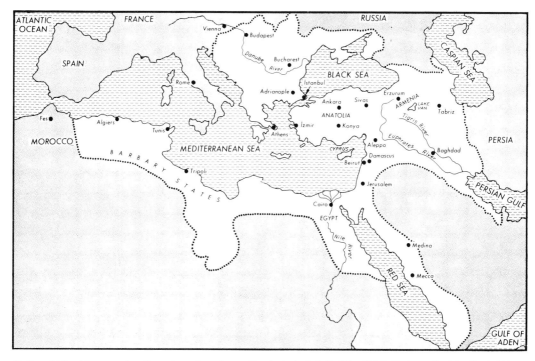

By the middle of the seventeenth century, the Ottoman Empire included all of the Middle East, much of the North African coast, and parts of Europe. Map taken from *The Area Handbook for the Republic of Turkey*, 1973.

Mamluk rule in 1517. The Turks ruled Lebanon until the end of World War I in 1918. From their far-off capital in Turkey, the Ottomans did little to develop Lebanon and allowed the local Maan family to rule the region.

The Maans belonged to the Druze religion (a secretive sect that developed from Islam in the eleventh century), but they were able to gather support from the Maronite Christians. Beginning in the Lebanon Mountains, the Maans extended their power east and west to include the Bekaa Valley and the coastal area.

Fakhr al-Din, whose reign began in 1593, was the strongest leader in the Maan family. He succeeded in unifying the diverse religious groups—Maronite Christians, Druze, Sunni Muslims, and Shiite Muslims —in the country. He also encouraged ties with Europe as well as a movement toward independence. The Turks eventually discovered Fakhr's liberation efforts and executed him in 1635.

This entrance to the palace at Beit al-Din leads to the private apartments used by the family of Bashir Shihab II in the early nineteenth century.

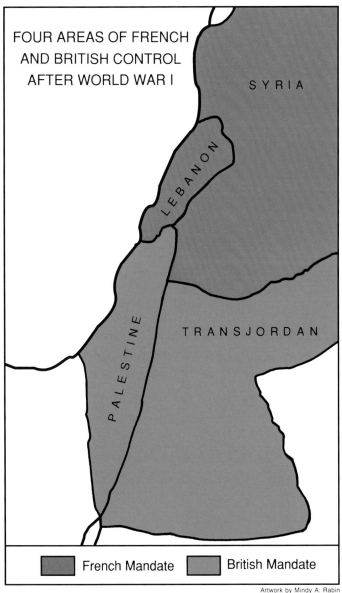

FOUR AREAS OF FRENCH
AND BRITISH CONTROL
AFTER WORLD WAR I

SYRIA

LEBANON

PALESTINE

TRANSJORDAN

French Mandate   British Mandate

Artwork by Mindy A. Rabin

After the Allied powers defeated the Turks in World War I, they divided up Turkish holdings. In the Middle East, Great Britain took control of Palestine and what would become Transjordan (now Israel and Jordan), and France occupied Lebanon and Syria.

The Ottoman Turks then entrusted another family, the Shihabs, to govern Lebanon. The Shihabs were Sunni Muslims who began their leadership in 1697. Maronite Christians supported the Shihab family just as they had the Maans. The succeeding years were prosperous and peaceful, and Lebanon's economy and population grew.

Like Fakhr al-Din, Bashir Shihab II had dreams of independence. Shihab allied himself with the Egyptian leader Muhammad Ali Pasha, who challenged Ottoman rule in 1831 and who ousted the Ottomans from Lebanon. Although free of Turkish control, the Shihab family governed harshly. Because the new regime increased taxes and forced men to serve in the army, the Maronites and the Druze revolted. In 1840 Ottoman and British forces turned Bashir Shihab II out of Lebanon.

Bitter hostilities and violence between Christians and Druze erupted during the 1840s. The Ottomans had encouraged tensions between the religious groups to prevent them from uniting and effectively working for independence. In 1842 several European nations suggested dividing Lebanon into a Christian area north of the Beirut-Damascus road and a Druze area to the south of it. This scheme failed because members of the dominant faith in each area attacked members of the minority religion.

The Ottomans, with the aid of European powers, intervened and installed a Christian governor—called a mutessarif—for the whole country. A 12-member council that represented all the religious groups in Lebanon assisted the Christian mutessarif. The governorship began in 1861 and continued until August 1915, when Ottoman military officers took direct control during World War I.

World War I and Its Aftermath

The Turks allied themselves with Germany during World War I, during which executions, famine, and disease caused thousands of deaths. Isolated from its Western European trading outlets, Lebanon's economy declined drastically. The Turks depleted much of Lebanon's remaining cedar forests, using the wood for fuel.

Britain—one of the victorious Allied powers—ended Turkish rule in Lebanon at the end of World War I. The Allies gathered at the war's conclusion and placed Lebanon under a French mandate. The French would help Lebanon set up a government until Lebanon was ready to govern itself independently.

The French mandate began in 1920, and the first Lebanese constitution went into effect in 1926. The Lebanese who ran the country under the guidance of the French commissioner for Lebanon had difficulty establishing Lebanese leadership. Several people held the presidency of Lebanon

over the next 20 years. But most of them were appointed by the French commissioner rather than by the Lebanese legislature, as called for by the constitution.

Under French guidance, the Lebanese economy grew strong once again. The government repaired and extended roads throughout the country and enlarged the port of Beirut. More schools were built, and agricultural practices were improved.

World War II and Independence

In 1943, during World War II, Lebanon gained its full independence from the French. General elections were held and the newly elected Chamber of Deputies (the Lebanese parliament) chose Bishara al-Khoury as president. Khoury, a Christian, invited Riad al-Solh, a Muslim, to become prime minister. The two leaders worked out the unwritten National Covenant that guides relations between Muslims and Christians in Lebanon.

The French briefly tried to reverse the flow of independence in 1943 by suspending the revised constitution and by arresting the government leaders. The Lebanese

Courtesy of R. D. Research

This five-piaster coin, minted after Lebanese independence in 1943, has Arabic writing on one side and French on the other.

31

people rioted, and foreign governments protested so strongly that the French relented, freeing the Lebanese leaders and putting the constitution into effect again.

In 1945, near the end of World War II, the Lebanese declared war on Germany and Japan. After the war, Lebanon became a charter member of both the United Nations (UN) and the Arab League.

In 1948 Israel established itself as an independent nation on Lebanon's southern border. Created to provide a national homeland for the Jewish people, Israel met great resistance from its Arab neighbors, including Lebanon. An Arab-Israeli war followed, after which Lebanon took in over 100,000 refugees who fled Palestine, the region from which the Jewish nation was carved. Tension in the Middle East and the resettlement of Palestinian refugees in Lebanon have affected almost every event in Lebanon's recent history.

Pan-Arabism

Tensions deepened between Christians, who had become Westernized, and Muslims, who were influenced by the Eastern, Arab world. In the late 1950s Gamal Abdel Nasser, president of Egypt, led a movement for Pan-Arabism, which envisioned strengthening and uniting the Arab world. Many Lebanese Muslims were drawn to Nasser and the Pan-Arabic cause.

When rebels overthrew the pro-Western government in Iraq, the Lebanese government feared a similar rebellion by those who were strongly pro-Arab in Lebanon. Camille Chamoun, Lebanon's president, asked for and received help from the

Courtesy of UNRWA

These two young Arab girls were among the first refugees from Palestine (the region in which Israel established its homeland in 1948). The Palestinian refugees lived in tents near Sidon for many years until the UN Relief and Works Agency (UNRWA) constructed more permanent structures in the camps.

Independent Picture Service

U.S. Marines landed on the coast of Lebanon in 1958 in response to former president Camille Chamoun's request for help. The president hoped that the U.S. presence would calm tensions between the Lebanese government and those who supported the Pan-Arabic movement.

United States. Several thousand U.S. Marines landed at the port of Beirut, and their presence helped restore order.

Lebanon, Israel, and Refugees

Although situated in the heart of what has become a Middle East trouble zone, Lebanon has attempted to remain neutral. Following the Arab-Israeli war in 1967—known as the Six-Day War—more refugees arrived in Lebanon.

In 1968 Israeli commandos destroyed a number of planes at the Beirut airport. The attack was in response to a Lebanese-based Palestinian raid on an Israeli airliner in Athens, Greece. As a result, Lebanon could no longer remain uninvolved in the growing Middle Eastern conflict.

Intense warfare also arose as Palestinian guerrilla fighters in Lebanese territory openly clashed with the Lebanese army. After a stalemate developed, the two sides entered into the Cairo Agreement, a

Independent Picture Service

Israeli soldiers raise their nation's flag on Mount Hermon during the Yom Kippur War in 1973. With each new Arab-Israeli conflict, more Palestinian refugees have arrived in Lebanon.

33

Refugee camps are built from cast-away materials and are often over-crowded. Because of widespread dissatisfaction among the refugees, the camps are recruiting grounds for the Palestine Liberation Organization (PLO).

compromise that established guidelines for the activities of the Palestinians within Lebanon. Many features of this agreement have been kept secret, but the result has been a weakening of the Lebanese government's control over its own territory. In addition, pressure from other Arab states in support of Palestinian activities mounted. Israel, on the other hand, sent forces across the Lebanese border to stop Palestinian attacks on Israeli towns.

In 1970 many Palestinian guerrilla fighters were driven out of Jordan and pushed into Lebanon, where they joined the 150,000 Palestinian refugees already there. The newly arrived Palestinians included many members of the Palestine Liberation Organization (PLO), which is dedicated

On several occasions, United Nations (UN) troops have acted as a peacekeeping force in Lebanon. Here, a group of UN soldiers fortifies one of its positions with sandbags.

to the establishment of a Palestinian homeland. The Lebanese attempted to keep tight control over the PLO, but they had little success. The PLO made up a powerful faction in southern Lebanon, and the continued activity of Palestinian guerrillas against Israel led to Israeli counterattacks across the border.

In October 1973 another Arab-Israeli war broke out when Egypt and Syria attacked Israel on the Jewish holy day of Yom Kippur. Known as the Yom Kippur War, the conflict saw fierce fighting between Syrian and Israeli troops near Lebanon's southeastern frontier. The Lebanese government did not become actively involved, however, even though PLO attacks from Lebanon on Israel led to renewed Israeli attacks on Lebanese territory.

In March 1978 Israel crossed into southern Lebanon to destroy the bases of the PLO. The United States pressured Israel to withdraw, and the UN sent a peacekeeping force to restore the government's control. The UN forces set up a 15-mile-wide buffer zone between the Israeli border and the PLO forces. The PLO, however, returned to the area and continued its attacks against Israel.

Civil War

During 1975 and 1976, battles erupted almost every day throughout Lebanon between several religious groups. The earlier

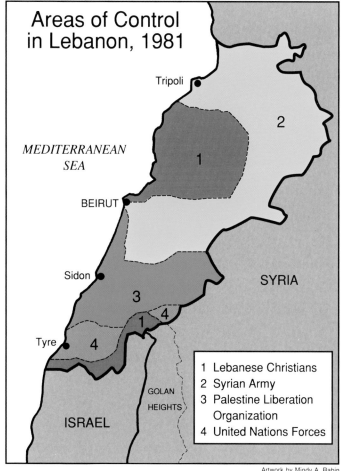

Areas of Control in Lebanon, 1981

Tripoli

MEDITERRANEAN SEA

2

1

BEIRUT

Sidon

3

SYRIA

1 4

Tyre

4

GOLAN HEIGHTS

ISRAEL

1 Lebanese Christians
2 Syrian Army
3 Palestine Liberation Organization
4 United Nations Forces

The territories controlled by the different factions within Lebanon frequently change. This map shows the areas under Lebanese Christian, Syrian, PLO, and UN control in 1981.

Artwork by Mindy A. Rabin

Israeli attacks had unsettled the population, especially in southern Lebanon, fanning resentments between Muslims and Christians and between both of these groups and the Palestinians. Civil war tore the country apart, and the central government nearly ceased to operate.

Religious subgroups formed their own militias to protect themselves and to correct the wrongs they felt had been committed against them. Foreign nations supplied the different groups with weapons, and the factions turned upon one another with previously unequaled fire-power.

The Lebanese and Syrian governments made a proposal to stop the fighting by increasing the parliamentary representation of the Muslim factions. The PLO rejected this solution because they hoped to directly control at least part of Lebanon. Syria responded by sending more of its troops to Beirut and to southern Lebanon. With Syrians placed between the main Christian and PLO armies, civil warfare had nearly ceased by the end of 1976.

The city of Beirut was split into a Christian eastern section and a Muslim western portion, and the country also was divided. Christians controlled the north, and to the south the combined Druze, Muslim, and Palestinian forces held authority. Although the civil war among roughly 100 small militias had ended, fighting among various Lebanese factions continued. The economic destruction in Lebanon resulting from the dispute was massive.

Photo by Religious News Service

Beginning in the 1970s, militia units fought one another throughout the city of Beirut. In January 1986, this Syrian-backed Christian force fired upon another Christian militia loyal to Lebanon's president Amin Gemayel.

Israeli troops entered Lebanon during 1982 to contain the PLO forces that were attacking Israel across its northern border. The Israelis eventually occupied Beirut and forced many PLO fighters to leave Lebanon.

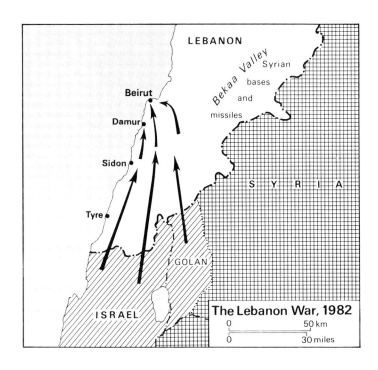

Israeli Invasion

On June 6, 1982, 75,000 Israeli troops invaded Lebanon with the goal of securing enough territory to stop the PLO raids on Israel. The Israelis pushed through southern Lebanon, and 15,000 PLO fighters retreated into Beirut. Eventually the PLO was put under siege in West Beirut. An international group of U.S., French, and Italian forces arrived and kept watch as the PLO leaders and troops were allowed to leave by sea for other Arab nations. The international forces left within two weeks after the PLO's departure in August 1982.

Bashir Gemayel was elected president of Lebanon that same August, only to be killed by a bomb at his Maronite party headquarters within a month. The day after his death, the Israeli army advanced into Beirut with the intention of preventing an outbreak of violence among the conflicting Muslim and Christian militias. Within two days the Israelis had taken the city.

Soon afterward, forces from France, Italy, and the United States returned to

Photo by Religious News Service

Yasir Arafat, born in Jerusalem in 1929, has been an active leader of the Palestinians. In 1968 Arafat was named chairperson of the PLO, becoming a chief organizer of PLO guerrilla activities. The 1982 seige of Beirut by the Israeli army drove Arafat, along with 15,000 PLO fighters, from Lebanon to other Arab nations.

At the Good Fence, an aid station located along the Lebanese-Israeli border, relief agencies from within Israel offer assistance to Lebanese civilians in need of food or medical attention.

Lebanon in an attempt to foster peace. Amin Gemayel was elected president in the month after his brother Bashir's death. Tension and conflict persisted as the people of Lebanon tried to resolve their continuing national crisis.

In February 1985 Israeli troops pulled out of Sidon in the face of growing pressure from Shiite Muslims. The Shiites no longer saw the Israelis as liberators from PLO dominance. Instead, the Muslims sought to establish themselves in power. By June 1985 the Israeli army had withdrawn from Lebanon. Subsequent attempts to forge a settlement between the rival Lebanese Christian and Muslim factions were complicated by the continual fighting and guerrilla actions, including a series of car bombings in Beirut and Tripoli.

Recent Events

When Muslim and Christian politicians could not decide on a new president in

Political posters, including one of President Gemayel, are attached to a barricade that lies across a Beirut street.

Dr. Elias Hrawi became the Lebanese president in 1989, a few days after his predecessor was assassinated. Hrawi has the difficult task of rebuilding a divided and heavily damaged nation.

September 1988, rival cabinets were set up by each of the religious groups. The Lebanese army, which is led by Christians, gained control over several Christian militias. In March 1989 street battles erupted again in Beirut. General Michel Aoun, the commander of the Lebanese army, attempted to drive the Syrian military from their bases in Lebanon.

In response to the fighting, members of the Arab League met in September 1989 to implement a cease-fire. Lebanese legislators met in Taif, Saudi Arabia, to draw up a "charter of national reconciliation." The Taif Agreement gave more power to a Lebanese cabinet of ministers and increased the number of seats in the National Assembly, the Lebanese legislature. In addition, Muslims and Christians were to have an equal number of seats in the country's cabinet and legislature.

Although it was opposed by General Aoun, the Taif Agreement gained the

Lebanon's flag was adopted in 1943, the year in which the nation achieved independence. The cedar tree, an ancient Lebanese symbol, signifies enduring strength. The red stripes represent the self-sacrifice needed for independence, and the field of white stands for Lebanon's desire for peace.

support of a majority of Lebanese legislators. The National Assembly met in early November to elect a new president, Rene Mouawad. Only 17 days after his election, however, Mouawad was assassinated. The legislature then elected Dr. Elias Hrawi to replace Mouawad. In the next year, the legislature ratified the new constitution, an action which led to the inauguration of the Second Lebanese Republic.

In the meantime, the Lebanese cabinet announced the removal of General Aoun as commander of the Lebanese army. In October 1990, Aoun was forced out of his stronghold in Beirut. After the Lebanese army extended its control to both East and West Beirut, the well-armed private militias abandoned the city.

As part of the Taif Agreement, open elections were held in the summer of 1992. Maronite Christians, who oppose Syria's presence in Lebanon, refused to participate in the elections. As a result, the voting brought a pro-Syrian majority to the Lebanese parliament. In addition, despite its pledge to withdraw after the elections, Syria has maintained its army in Lebanon. Conflict among Lebanon's political and religious factions is again threatening the country's peaceful rebuilding. Another problem is occurring in South Lebanon, where the Israeli army occupies a security zone along the border between the two countries. Since the end of the civil war, several skirmishes have erupted between the Israeli army and the forces of Hezbollah, a militant Shiite Muslim group.

The Government

Lebanon's constitution was amended after the Taif Agreement of 1989. The president

Photo © Al Jawad/SIPA Press

In 1988, these Syrian soldiers patrolled a Beirut neighborhood during heavy fighting between two Lebanese militias. Although fighting has ceased in Beirut, Syrian forces still control Lebanon's Bekaa Valley.

Although Lebanese life has been fractured by unresolved strife, the political process still takes place. Here, campaign posters line city streets in support of candidates competing in a legislative election.

of the republic, who is chosen by the legislature, serves a term of six years and may not be immediately re-elected to another term. Lebanese citizens 21 years of age and older vote for the members of the legislature. The cabinet and a prime minister are appointed by the president of the republic, and these ministers are responsible to the legislature. In October 1992, President Hrawi appointed Rafik Hariri, a Sunni Muslim politician, as Prime Minister. Since then, Hariri has led the efforts to rebuild Lebanon.

EXECUTIVE POWER

According to the unwritten National Covenant that modifies the constitution, the president is chosen from the ranks of Maronite Christians, and the cabinet is headed by a prime minister who must be a Sunni Muslim. The cabinet is equally divided between Christian and Muslim ministers. Governors administer Lebanon's five provinces.

The president and the cabinet approve and enforce laws passed by the legislature. The president also has the power to adjourn the legislature or to dissolve it and force a new general election. However, the executive leader must seek the approval of the cabinet to dismiss a minister or to ratify an international treaty.

LEGISLATIVE POWER

In August, 1990, the Lebanese legislature, known as the National Assembly, voted to increase the number of seats in the body from 99 to 108. According to the Taif Agreement, the seats are to be equally divided among Christians and Muslims. The legislature holds two sessions yearly, in the spring and fall. The normal legislative term is four years, but the term has been repeatedly extended since the 1970s.

JUDICIAL POWER

The Lebanese court system has three levels. Both criminal and civil cases are tried originally in a court of first instance. where cases are decided by a single judge. The next higher level is a court of appeal, which is composed of three-judge panels. A court of cassation is the highest court in Lebanon, and cases that come before it are also decided by a panel. Religious communities have their own courts for deciding marriage, divorce, guardianship, inheritance, and religious matters.

41

Maronite monks follow in the footsteps of their fifth-century A.D. founder, Saint Maron. This monk says his prayers in the Syriac language and follows a way of life that began when the first colony of Maronite monks lived and taught in the mountains of northern Lebanon.

Courtesy of Lebanese Information and Research Center

3) The People

Although records show 3.9 million people in the Republic of Lebanon, frequent emigration makes this figure only an estimate. About 87 percent of the population live in urban areas, and, at the current population growth rate, the number of people in the country is expected to double in 33 years.

Religion

Religious groups in Lebanon are the basis for the country's political divisions. Each group has many subgroups, and each of these has its own militia. The groups made many different alliances over the years, often finding themselves fighting those with whom they recently had ties.

CHRISTIANS

The Maronites are the major Christian group in Lebanon. In the seventh century the Maronites entered a period of controversy with other Christians over teachings about the will of Jesus. Maronites believed in Monothelitism (from the Greek words meaning single will). The Maronites taught that Jesus had one will made up of human and divine parts. The larger Christian church, which said that Jesus had both a divine and a human will, condemned the Maronite teaching.

The Maronites retreated into the remote regions of the Lebanon Mountains to practice their faith without persecution. Their dispute with the Christian Church was resolved in the twelfth century, when the Maronites became allies of the European crusaders. Later, under Ottoman rule, the Maronites grew stronger and expanded into some of the coastal areas of Lebanon.

In 1943 the National Covenant recognized the Maronites as the biggest religious and political group within Lebanon. This status gave them the largest representation in the legislature of Lebanon and determined that the president must belong to the Maronite group. Other Christian groups include the Greek Orthodox, Armenian Orthodox, Greek Catholics, and Roman Catholics.

MUSLIMS

Muslims follow the faith of Islam, a word that means submission to God's will. Begun in the seventh century by Muhammad, Islam has two main sects—the Sunnis and the Shiites, who both follow the central practices of the faith. Muslims pray five times daily facing in the direction of Mecca, the place of Muhammad's birth. They are called to prayer by muezzins (criers), who chant from minarets (tall towers) to announce the hour of prayer.

Muslims pray together in mosques when they can, especially on Friday, the holy day of the week. Mosques have no statues or pictures because Islam prohibits religious images. Muslims fast from sunrise to sunset during the month of Ramadan, the ninth month of the Islamic calendar. If possible, the faithful make a pilgrimage to Mecca once in their lifetime.

A Christian church in Antilyas, a few miles east of Beirut, dominates the town square. Although a large Sunni Muslim population lives near Tripoli, the northern section of the Lebanon Mountains is a heavily Christian area made up mainly of Maronites and members of the Greek Orthodox Church.

43

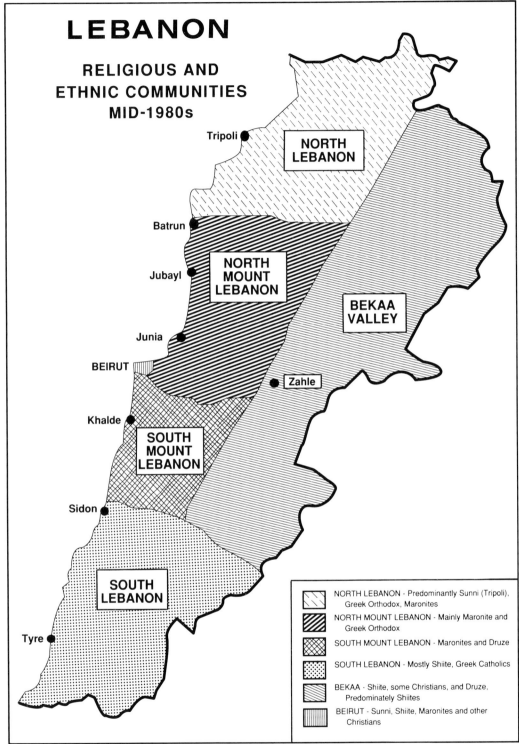

LEBANON

RELIGIOUS AND ETHNIC COMMUNITIES MID-1980s

Tripoli

NORTH LEBANON

Batrun

NORTH MOUNT LEBANON

Jubayl

Junia

BEIRUT

BEKAA VALLEY

Zahle

Khalde

SOUTH MOUNT LEBANON

Sidon

SOUTH LEBANON

Tyre

	NORTH LEBANON - Predominantly Sunni (Tripoli), Greek Orthodox, Maronites
	NORTH MOUNT LEBANON - Mainly Maronite and Greek Orthodox
	SOUTH MOUNT LEBANON - Maronites and Druze
	SOUTH LEBANON - Mostly Shiite, Greek Catholics
	BEKAA - Shiite, some Christians, and Druze, Predominately Shiites
	BEIRUT - Sunni, Shiite, Maronites and other Christians

Artwork by Mindy A. Rabin

Although the location of religious strongholds has shifted somewhat in the twentieth century, this map shows the geographic distribution of religious communities in the 1980s.

Members of a Lebanese Muslim family gather with their young children to share sweet Arabic coffee, a beverage that is served in Arab households in many nations.

Although Sunni Muslims are the majority Islamic sect in the world, in Lebanon they are fewer in number than the Shiite group. Since the death of Muhammad, the main point of division between Sunnis and Shiites has centered on how leadership within Islam is to be determined. Yet the conflict over leadership is only part of what separates Sunnis and Shiites in Lebanon. Sunnis are economically more successful than the Shiites and often wield more political power. In Lebanon, most Shiites are low-income farmers. Consequently, they often see themselves as underprivileged and oppressed. In recent years Hezbollah and Amal, another militant Shiite organization, have become a political voice for Lebanese Shiites, with several members serving in the Lebanese legislature.

DRUZE

The Druze are a fiercely independent and secretive religious group that have

These Lebanese women are wearing traditional Arab clothing. A growing movement favoring strict adherence to Islamic laws encourages women to cover themselves in full-length garb as a sign of modesty.

45

Courtesy of UNRWA

During a lull in the fighting, a Palestinian woman washes dishes in an alley of the Burj al-Barajneh refugee camp, while her children play nearby.

Courtesy of United Nations

An elderly Lebanese woman wearing a traditional Muslim veil stands in front of her home in Beirut.

been a major factor in shaping Lebanon's history. Originating as a development of Shiite Islam in the eleventh century, the Druze derive their name from a mystic named Ismail al-Darazi. Al-Darazi was a follower of Al-Hakim, whom the Druze believe was an earthly presence of God. The Druze in Lebanon are a very tightly knit minority of about 300,000 people.

Palestinian Refugees

Lebanon has taken in three major waves of Palestinian refugees—after Israel became a nation in 1948, after the Six-Day War in 1967, and after the civil war in Jordan in 1970. The 500,000 refugees live in camps near Beirut and in southern Lebanon but have neither blended into Lebanese society nor received citizenship. Although they are mostly Sunni Muslims, they remain a separate group and do not figure in the balance of the religious factions.

Most Palestinians live in refugee camps, where living conditions are very difficult. Food and medicine are scarce, and housing is only makeshift. Those who live in the camps are the political base and recruiting ground for the various factions of the PLO. The refugee camps have been attacked and besieged by Israeli, Christian, and Shiite Muslim forces.

Status of Women

Although Arab countries seldom allow women to work in offices, in Lebanon's urban areas women hold responsible positions in radio, television, medicine, and science. Ninety percent of Lebanese women are literate, which is a higher rate than in most Arab countries. The influence of the French culture in the early part of the twentieth century contributed to the change in the status of women in Lebanon.

Some Muslim women have given up the Islamic custom of wearing a facial veil. Others, however, still appear on city streets covered from head to foot in black burkas, revealing only their eyes. These women are likely to be members of conservative Islamic groups and are returning to more traditional customs.

Urban Life

Four out of five Lebanese live in urban areas. For 5,000 years or more, different peoples and cultures have mixed in these cities and ports. But in the 1970s and 1980s, guerrilla activity and warfare damaged and disrupted Lebanon's cities.

Beirut is an example of the extreme changes in urban life that occurred during the country's civil war. Once a fashionable, modern city with many restaurants and coffeehouses, Beirut was divided by a fortified barrier and occupied by well-armed, rival militias. The city's lively daytime activity came to a halt as businesses withdrew from the city, and hotels and restaurants in West Beirut closed. Sniping, bombing and kidnapping became daily occurrences.

The halt in the war in the early 1990s allowed city officials to clear debris, tear down ruined buildings, and prepare for Beirut's rebuilding. The suqs, or open-air markets, have reappeared and offer whatever produce and goods are available. Life in the other cities has not been affected as drastically as it has been in Beirut.

Rural Life

Lebanese farming villages are often organized according to clans or families, and intermarriage among families often occurs. Those who move to the cities still identify themselves with their village. The leader of the village solves the problems and disputes that arise in the community. Families usually own the land on which they grow crops, and men and boys do most of the field work.

Warfare disrupted rural life in much of southern Lebanon. The PLO often taxed

Courtesy of Lebanese Information and Research Center

In an effort to live in relative safety, this Beirut woman has moved her kitchen to the basement of her house.

Independent Picture Service

Rural homes are usually made of limestone with a flat earthen roof. Many homes have one main room that is subdivided by wooden cabinets or curtains.

47

Courtesy of Lebanese Information and Research Center

Suqs (markets) offer fruits, vegetables, and grains as well as hand-made baskets and other items. The availability of goods has become greater since the fighting ended.

village families to support their cause, and roads fell under the control of various militias. Farmers were prevented from planting, harvesting, and transporting their produce. Since the cease-fire, however, the Lebanese government has gained control over most of the country's rural districts and roadways.

Food

In times of peace and when foods are readily available, Lebanon has a rich culinary tradition. *Mezzé,* the Lebanese smorgasbord, is a gigantic selection of hot and cold appetizers that includes spicy salads, mashed beans mixed with olive oil, and zesty meatballs with nuts. Shrimp and seafood are also served, along with sausage rolls in crisp pastry and stuffed grapevine leaves.

Shish kebab is a popular Middle Eastern dish of skewered cubes of lamb, green pep-

Courtesy of Catholic Near East Welfare Association

A young Lebanese boy sits patiently beside a stack of freshly baked *khobez,* the flat, round bread that is a staple of most Lebanese meals.

48

This Lebanese cook is making kibbe, one of the nation's distinctive foods. Composed of chopped lamb and bulgur (cracked wheat), kibbe is often baked and eaten in square-shaped portions.

pers, and onions. Lebanese bread—hot, flat rounds of wheat called *khobez*—is one of the nation's staple foods. Meals start with appetizers such as *hummos*—chickpeas mashed with sesame oil and garlic —eggplant salad, tabbouleh (chopped tomatoes, scallions, parsley, and cracked wheat), and stuffed grape leaves. Main dishes often are made with lamb cooked in various ways and are almost always served with rice. Dessert often includes baklava—a flaky pastry that is filled with chopped nuts and honey.

A quick lunch may be a slice of hot ground meat rolled with peppers in a piece of khobez. Barbequed chicken is popular and sells out quickly in the towns and villages. Local wines often are served with meals.

Health

Lebanon trains a relatively large proportion of medical personnel in the Middle East, although the number of people in training has declined since the civil war. The Lebanese hold doctors and nurses in high esteem, but the large cities attract the majority of these professionals. In rural Lebanon, a serious lack of doctors and nurses and inadequate medical facilities hamper health care. In the countryside,

Courtesy of Catholic Near East Welfare Association

A mother brings her young daughter to one of the crowded clinics in Beirut for medical attention. The child burned her arm in a fire started by a bombardment in her neighborhood.

midwives schooled in village traditions are the main medical support, not only for women giving birth but also for many of those with illnesses.

Typhoid, dysentery, hepatitis (an inflamed liver), and schistosomiasis (a liver disease caused by parasites) are prevalent in Lebanon. Out of every 1,000 Lebanese infants, 37 die within one year of birth. Although this figure is high by Western standards, it is much better than that of many countries in western Asia. The life expectancy of 70 years of age compares well with the western Asian average of 66 years of age.

Education

Lebanon has been an intellectual center of the Arab world for centuries. The literacy rate during the early 1990s was near 90 percent, and, even amid political turmoil, the government is working to increase funding for education.

Primary education is compulsory, and 93 percent of Lebanese children attend school. Many schools are privately run, creating difficulties for low-income Lebanese who want to educate their children. Since the 1960s, the government has been trying to increase the number of both primary and secondary public schools.

Almost all secondary schools are privately run. Because it offers a broader education, secondary school is preferred over vocational training. Lebanese families value education so highly that they will make significant sacrifices to send their children to secondary school. Earning a diploma at the secondary level brings prestige to the whole family as well as to the individual.

Of three main universities, the American University of Beirut, founded in 1866 by Protestant missionaries, is the best known. It offers programs in the arts and sciences, medicine, engineering, and agriculture. Many regard the American

50

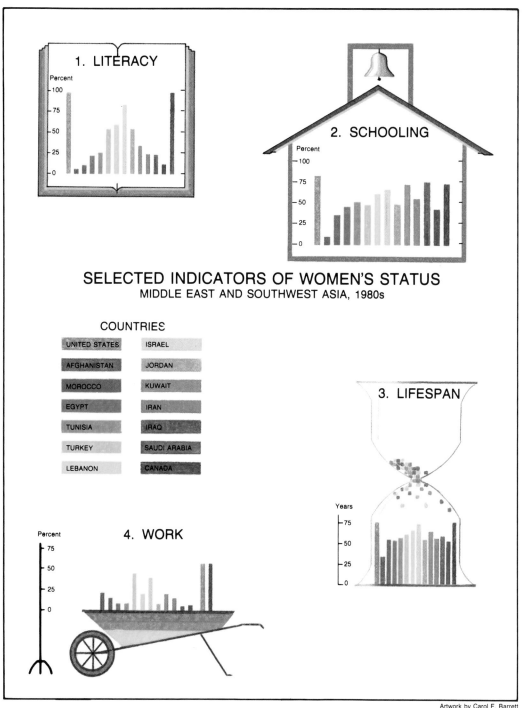

SELECTED INDICATORS OF WOMEN'S STATUS
MIDDLE EAST AND SOUTHWEST ASIA, 1980s

COUNTRIES

UNITED STATES	ISRAEL
AFGHANISTAN	JORDAN
MOROCCO	KUWAIT
EGYPT	IRAN
TUNISIA	IRAQ
TURKEY	SAUDI ARABIA
LEBANON	CANADA

Artwork by Carol F. Barrett

Depicted in this chart are factors relating to the status of women in the Middle East and southwest Asia. Graph 1, labeled Literacy, shows the percentage of adult women who can read and write. Graph 2 illustrates the proportion of school-aged girls who actually attend elementary and secondary schools. Graph 3 depicts the life expectancy of female babies at birth. Graph 4 shows the percentage of women in the income-producing work force. Data taken from *Women in the World: An International Atlas*, 1986 and from *Women . . . A World Survey*, 1985.

University as the most influential institution of higher education in the Middle East. During the recent warfare, however, the university's facilities were damaged extensively. Faculty and students also suffered in the turmoil. Although the school was often closed during the fighting, it reopened in November 1991, as the country regained its political stability.

St. Joseph's University, founded by Roman Catholics in 1875, has schools of engineering and medicine, as well as a special institute dedicated to Middle Eastern studies. The Lebanese University, also in Beirut, stresses law, political science, and the arts.

Each mosque and church in Lebanon is not only a place of worship but also of education. Classes teach children to study the Koran (the Muslim book of sacred writings) or the Christian Bible. In this way, instructors pass on the cultural traditions of their religions.

The Arts

Most Lebanese children start music lessons in kindergarten, and often they perform the country's folk music at school concerts. Arab singers in the Bekaa Valley are often accompanied by the rebab, a stringed instrument played with a bow. Rebab performers play variations on a melody, and a singer and an instrumentalist alternate in performing the music. Besides folk music, students also learn Western classical music.

Many theaters are dedicated exclusively to traditional drama, consisting of puppet shows or romantic plays based on traditional Arab folktales. At Baalbek in the Bekaa Valley, actors perform folklore dramas at the annual International Festival, an event that drama and music lovers from around the world have attended since it began in 1956. Using the ancient ruins of Roman temples as a backdrop, the programs include French and English dramat-

Courtesy of UNRWA

These Palestinian students at a UN-sponsored school in Beirut enthusiastically participate in their classes. Many schools in the capital have been damaged, and some run on double shifts to accommodate the growing Lebanese and refugee student populations. The UN Relief Agency provides schooling for some 35,000 Palestinian primary and intermediate students.

At an open-air suq in southern Lebanon, a potter exhibits his wares to a customer.

A weaver *(left)* makes distinctive Lebanese cloth on a hand loom that has belonged to his family for generations. Near Tripoli in northern Lebanon, craftspeople produce delicately engraved copper trays and ewers *(above)*.

ic productions, as well as symphonic music and ballet.

Village artisans practice the arts and crafts of Lebanon. Between planting and harvesting seasons, many village children learn how to hammer brass, create leather goods, or make pottery. The Lebanese ex-

cel in the goldsmith's art, and throughout the Bab-Idris section of Beirut jewelers work on intricate patterns. Many Lebanese towns are famous for a special craft. Jezzin in the mountains, for example, is famed for the delicate crafting of bone-handled knives.

A farmer and his family pack their tomato crop to take it to market. Lebanon's farming regions are located along the coastal plain, in the lower reaches of the mountains, and in the fertile Bekaa Valley.

4) The Economy

Unlike many other countries that have relied on agriculture for economic survival, Lebanon has traditionally based its economy on a variety of activities. With the country's good ports and transportation links, commercial trade has always been Lebanon's economic strength. During the civil war, however, the economy declined as productivity fell drastically and new investment nearly ceased. But the Lebanese government has launched a program to rebuild the country's shattered economy.

Industry

Before the civil war, Lebanon was expanding its facilities for industrial production. The country produced abundant electric power from hydroelectric plants. A well-kept highway system and large, modern seaports and airports provided communication, shipping, and transportation facilities. To increase the work force, well-equipped technical schools were established. In order to encourage industrial expansion, the state did not tax businesses

54

that contributed to the country's development. The turmoil of civil war, however, ended foreign investment, hampered progress, and in some areas destroyed industrial production completely.

The textile industry produces goods ranging from raw thread to finished silks and woolens. Clothing is mass-produced, and workers make high-quality shoes and handbags. Many small furniture factories produce long-lasting and stylish goods. The Lebanese are adept at design, and buyers from the East and the West seek their leather, wood, and paper products.

Chocolate is a specialty in Tripoli, and it is exported either as candy or cookies. Many U.S. soft drink companies have established huge plants in Lebanon that employ thousands of Lebanese. Stonemasonry and brick making are also important industries, as is the production of plastic and rubber.

This potter combines the centuries-old tools and techniques of his trade with a modern convenience—an electrically powered potter's wheel.

Beirut's international airport is one of Lebanon's central transportation hubs. Many foreign countries have resumed flights to Beirut after suspending them throughout the 1980s.

Independent Picture Service

Before they were destroyed by warfare in the region, these pipes carried oil from Saudi Arabia across southern Lebanon to ships in the Mediterranean Sea.

One of Lebanon's greatest economic resources was the Trans-Arabian Pipeline Company with headquarters at Sidon. The Trans-Arabian Pipeline also represents an example of the severity of the current economic disaster. The pipeline formed a modern trade route running through the Arabian Peninsula—across northern Saudi Arabia, Jordan, Syria, and Lebanon—carrying crude oil from the Saudi oil fields to the eastern Mediterranean Sea. The overland journey of 900 miles greatly shortened the thousands of miles the oil once had to travel by sea to reach the same destination. This shortcut brought economic gain and new development to the pipeline-carrying countries.

But the pipeline has stopped operating in southern Lebanon. This event is the combined result of the civil war, the Israeli invasion, and the continuing armed conflicts in Lebanon—as well as the war between Iran and Iraq. The loss of this resource is a tremendous blow to Lebanon's economy.

Independent Picture Service

By losing the use of its oil pipeline, Lebanon's economy was deprived of a major money-making activity. The Trans-Arabian Pipeline terminal at Sidon no longer feeds oil to offshore tankers, and the oil facilities are either destroyed or idle.

Grapevines in Lebanon climb upward with the help of sticks and an overhead trellis. In this way, the fruit receives the full benefit of the region's hot climate.

Agriculture

In the Bekaa Valley, agriculture occupies about 20 percent of the labor force. Despite its small area, Lebanon has a wide variety of crops. Much of the cultivated land is given over to subtropical and temperate-zone fruits. Apples, grapes, olives, and tobacco grow easily. Lebanon is important among the Mediterranean citrus-producing countries, harvesting about 250,000 tons of fruit each year, much of which is exported to Arab countries.

The Green Plan, an agricultural development scheme, encourages Lebanese farmers in the mountains to establish terraces, or tiered slopes, to increase the amount of farmable land in the region.

Sunflowers grow well in the bright sun of the Bekaa Valley and may be used to make oil or soap.

57

Because of the range of climate, terrain, and altitude, summer and winter fruits and vegetables are always available. Before the civil war, Lebanon's agriculture was undergoing a renewal project, known as the Green Plan, which was initiated to conserve and improve the soil. The plan included planting trees to combat erosion, training qualified personnel, and making it easier for land developers to secure funding.

Some Lebanese also grow cannabis for hashish and opium poppies for heroin. As the Lebanese government lost control of its territory, this illegal activity increased. Since 1989, however, there have been

Lebanon's potato crop has made a comeback since the civil war of 1975 and 1976, when farmers had too few seed potatoes to plant in their fields. This harvest is from a farm near Zahlé in the Bekaa Valley.

Courtesy of FAO

With the Anti-Lebanon Mountains in the background, a harvesting machine unearths potatoes for workers to gather.

Courtesy of FAO

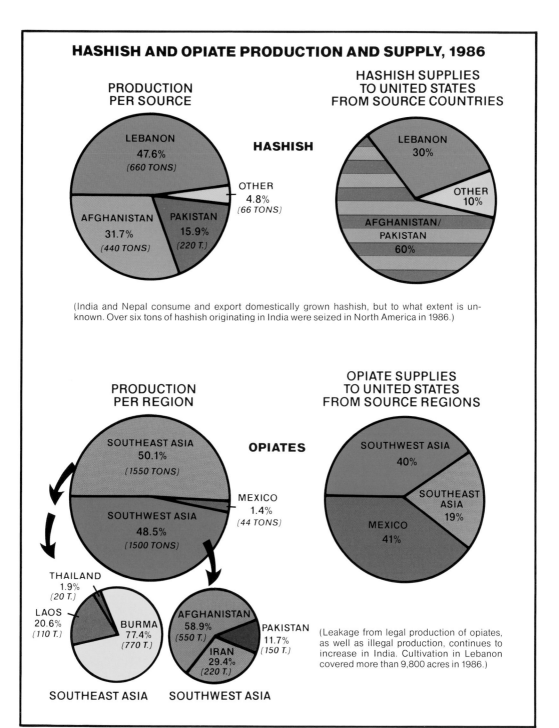

HASHISH AND OPIATE PRODUCTION AND SUPPLY, 1986

PRODUCTION PER SOURCE

HASHISH

HASHISH SUPPLIES TO UNITED STATES FROM SOURCE COUNTRIES

LEBANON
47.6%
(660 TONS)

OTHER
4.8%
(66 TONS)

AFGHANISTAN
31.7%
(440 TONS)

PAKISTAN
15.9%
(220 T.)

LEBANON
30%

OTHER
10%

AFGHANISTAN/
PAKISTAN
60%

(India and Nepal consume and export domestically grown hashish, but to what extent is unknown. Over six tons of hashish originating in India were seized in North America in 1986.)

PRODUCTION PER REGION

OPIATES

OPIATE SUPPLIES TO UNITED STATES FROM SOURCE REGIONS

SOUTHEAST ASIA
50.1%
(1550 TONS)

MEXICO
1.4%
(44 TONS)

SOUTHWEST ASIA
48.5%
(1500 TONS)

SOUTHWEST ASIA
40%

SOUTHEAST
ASIA
19%

MEXICO
41%

THAILAND
1.9%
(20 T.)

LAOS
20.6%
(110 T.)

BURMA
77.4%
(770 T.)

AFGHANISTAN
58.9%
(550 T.)

PAKISTAN
11.7%
(150 T.)

IRAN
29.4%
(220 T.)

SOUTHEAST ASIA

SOUTHWEST ASIA

(Leakage from legal production of opiates, as well as illegal production, continues to increase in India. Cultivation in Lebanon covered more than 9,800 acres in 1986.)

Artwork by Elizabeth Pilon

These pie charts depict data about both the production and U.S. supplies of two kinds of drugs. Hashish is a substance taken from the *Cannabis sativa* plant, which also is a source of marijuana. Opiates are drugs that come from opium poppies *(Papaver somniferum)*, mostly in the refined forms of opium and heroin. The production pies *(left)* cover the percentages estimated to be manufactured by each country or region. The pies depicting U.S. supplies *(right)* illustrate only percentages that arrive in the United States. They do not include amounts used within source countries or regions, nor do they illustrate percentages that go to other parts of the world. Data taken from the *NNICC Report, 1985–1986* compiled by the U.S. Drug Enforcement Administration, Washington, D.C.

several crackdowns on opium-growing in the Bekaa Valley. As a result, the acreage devoted to opium poppies has decreased dramatically.

Transportation

With only about 260 miles of railroad track and no navigable rivers, roads are Lebanon's main means of transportation. Four thousand miles of paved roads crisscross the country, with another 500 miles of unpaved roadways. One of the two main routes goes from Syria in the north, along the coast through the major coastal cities, to the Israeli border in the south. The other major highway stretches from Beirut, through the Lebanon Mountains and the Bekaa Valley, across the Anti-Lebanon Mountains to Damascus, Syria.

Independent Picture Service

In rural areas, donkeys still carry goods and provide transportation.

Courtesy of Embassy of Lebanon/Yetenekian

Although heavily damaged during the civil war of the 1970s and 1980s, the port of Beirut remains a mainstay of the Lebanese economy.

A worker sifts through a trough of olives before they are pressed to extract their oil. Lebanon's high-quality olive oil has long been a major export.

Lebanese fishermen who work off the northern Mediterranean coast inspect their fish traps. Fish are a small but important part of the Lebanese export economy.

Finance and Trade

Lebanon owed its previous reputation as the financial capital of the Middle East to its relative political and financial stability, as well as to its lack of banking regulations. Foreign governments (especially Arab nations) and individuals operated with great freedom in Lebanon's financial district. A 1966 crisis in Lebanon's largest bank prompted government regulation of banks. This move, along with the crisis of civil war and the continuing international conflict, has drastically altered the country's finance industry. Many foreign investors have taken their money out of Lebanese banks.

Lebanon's principal exports are fruits, vegetables, textiles, metal products, precious metals, jewelry, and coins. A large percentage of these items go to Saudi Arabia, Iraq, Italy, Switzerland, Syria, and Kuwait. Lebanon imports machinery, consumer goods, and petroleum products from Italy, France, the United States, West Germany, and Saudi Arabia. Lebanon imports far more than it exports, which increases the national debt.

Antelias, about 10 miles northeast of Beirut on the Mediterranean Sea, has continued to develop even during the strife that has engulfed the nation. This office complex was still under construction in the mid-1980s.

Warfare and the threat of terrorist activity seriously hampered banking and foreign trade in Lebanon. In hopes that a cease-fire will hold, the Lebanese government has hired foreign firms to rebuild downtown Beirut and the city's financial district.

Future Challenges

Lebanon's people have reason to hope that the civil war that ravaged their country in the 1970s and 1980s has come to an end. Private militias have withdrawn from Beirut, and a general cease-fire is in effect.

Although the Taif Agreement has given the nation a new constitution, the people of Lebanon are still divided along religious lines. In addition, the presence of a large force of Syrian troops has deterred Lebanon's politicians from taking strong action on the nation's economic problems.

The Lebanese have endured many hardships throughout their long history, which gives them hope that they will overcome their current difficulties. If the Lebanese can achieve unity and stability, their country will be able to return to its traditional role as a business crossroads between Asia, Africa, and Europe.

Young Lebanese boys play a game of war on the floor of one of their homes.

In a devastated section of war-torn Lebanon, winding streets pass in front of ruined houses whose yards are overgrown with untended vegetation.

A donkey takes its rider through the winding streets of a village in the Lebanon Mountains. The ladders standing next to many homes are used to climb to the flat roofs, which are often used as elevated patios.

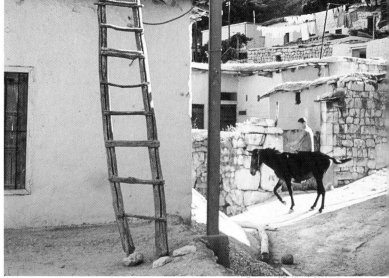

Index